CHERYL

Amma Asante

message from phil redmond

GRANGE HILL

Hi there!

Look out for lots of new things happening in Grange Hill during 1988 starting with this new-style annual which I hope you will enjoy reading, doing the puzzles, and taking part in some of the ideas.

Some of you will just be starting Secondary School. Let me know how your experiences compare with those of Grange Hill's new first years whom you will be meeting in Series 11 when it starts in January.

Last year we said a sad farewell to some very special people involved in Grange Hill and although they may be too old to be in the show we know they, like us, will never be too old to watch it.

I often get asked about ex-Grange Hill pupils and we had the chance to meet up with some of them again when past and present pupils played for the Grange Hill football teams in the 1987 Soap Cup. We saw Duane, Stewpot and Pogo playing alongside Danny, Zammo, and Gonch, and thanks to a brilliant goal by Duane, we managed to draw with Eastenders. The Grange Hill girls kept their end up when they won their match against the Brookside girls. It was all in aid of the NSPCC and hopefully will become another annual event to look forward to.

Keep sending me details of your own experiences and then see if you can recognise yourself when I turn them into Grange Hill episodes.

Phil

GRANGE HILL

ANNUAL 1988

CONTENTS

Published in Great Britain by World International Publishing Limited,
An Egmont Company, Egmont House, PO Box 111, Great Ducie Street,
Manchester M60 3BL.
ISBN 7235 6818 9

Printed in Italy

GETTING EVEN

It was dinner hour at Grange Hill. In the bushes close to Mr Griffiths' shed, Ziggy Greaves and his mate Robbie Wright crouched and waited. From the playground behind them came the sounds of kids playing football, fighting and fooling around. Over the top of it all was the crackle and static of Imelda Davis' radio turned up full tilt. The sound of it put Ziggy's nerves on edge and made him grit his teeth together, for it made him think about Imelda. And every time he thought about Imelda he felt sick. Sick and angry.

The girl was just an idiot, thought Ziggy. I mean a bit of mischief was just a bit of mischief. It was fun. And teachers were always fair game. But somehow, with Imelda, it was different. It wasn't even as if she ever seemed to get a laugh out of any of the aggro that she caused.

Like the other day when their class had been at the swimming pool with Mr Walker and Mrs Reagan. Imelda, as usual, had had a note from home saying that she couldn't do any swimming that week, and Mrs Reagan and Mr Walker had told her to sit upstairs and watch. Both teachers had been so busy with their groups – Mrs Reagan teaching the non-swimmers how to kick in the shallow end, Mr Walker and his advanced group diving for a rubber brick and treading water in their pyjamas in the deep end – that neither had noticed when Imelda had slipped through the door that led down from the spectators' gallery.

But Ziggy had. Which was how he'd known who to blame when they'd gone back to their changing rooms from the pool and found all their clothes underneath the shower. Of course, Mr Walker and Mrs Reagan had both asked Imelda what she knew about it, and of course, Imelda had been sullen, said she knew nothing about it, and accused both teachers of picking on her.

Only Ziggy knew better. He'd almost told both the games teachers that he'd seen Imelda sneaking downstairs halfway through the lesson, but even when he looked at his sopping wet trousers and the brown, purple and yellow felt-tip stains on his white shirt, he couldn't bring himself to sneak on her. Instead, he'd decided to get his own revenge, and he had spent most of his time since trying to think of some way he could get his own back.

As often happened, it had been Robbie who had eventually come up with a plan. Which was why the two of them were crouched in the bushes outside the caretaker's hut waiting for Mr Griffiths to finish the potted beef sandwiches and Kit Kat that his good lady wife packed for his lunch every Thursday.

Suddenly, the door of the hut opened and Mr Griffiths emerged. He paused to lock the large steel padlock that Mrs McClusky insisted he fit to the door after the trouble that Harriet the donkey had caused the previous term, and then strode away in the direction of the playing fields.

"OK, Robbie," whispered Ziggy, "this is our chance."

"Er, are you sure this is such a good idea?" asked Robbie nervously.

"It was your idea, wasn't it, you idiot?" demanded Ziggy as they hurried across to the back of the shed.

"Yeah, I know that," said Robbie, as he watched Ziggy cup his hands together to make a step up, "but it was just an idea. Shouldn't we wait a bit and then maybe . . ."

"Oh just shut up and get in there!" said Ziggy impatiently, hoisting Robbie up to the open window and then watching him wriggle through. There was a loud clattering sound as Robbie fell headfirst downward on top of Mr Griffiths' workbench. Ziggy pressed his face to the glass and peered inside. Robbie was pulling a paintbrush handle from up his nostril. His chin and the front of his blazer were covered in yellow turpentine.

"Come on, Robbie, hurry!" Ziggy urged, as he saw that Mr Griffiths had almost finished marking out the hockey pitch. Inside, Robbie was busy searching through the caretaker's tool box. Moments later he was scrambling back up to the fanlight above the window and he handed Ziggy a screwdriver, a pair of pliers, and an adjustable spanner. Then he followed after them, head first. He caught his belt buckle on the window catch and Ziggy reached up, grabbed his mate's arms and tugged. There was a tearing sound and the two of them tumbled to the ground in a heap.

"You don't half stink!" complained Ziggy, as they got to their feet and hurried away.

"So would you if you'd fallen into a pot of dirty paintbrushes," observed Robbie, trying to wipe the paint from his blazer and pull his jumper down over the tear in his trousers as he followed Ziggy toward the school.

The two of them made their way into the almost empty buildings. Ziggy led the way up the stairs and then along the corridor that led to the science department. He peered through the glass door to Mr Gayle's classroom and then, seeing that there was no one in, tried the door. It opened silently and the two schoolboys went inside.

"Okay, let's get to work," said Ziggy, and with the screwdriver, pliers, and spanner they set to work loosening all the nuts, bolts and screws in Imelda Davis' desk.

"I just had a thought, Ziggy," said Robbie, when they were halfway through their task.

"Yeah? What's that?" asked his companion.

"Well how do we know Imelda's going to be sitting here this afternoon?" asked Robbie.

Ziggy thought for a while. "Easy," he said eventually. "It's where she sits normally, isn't it?" Robbie nodded. "Then you sit there this afternoon," said Ziggy.

"But she'll go after me if I do that, won't she?" asked Robbie, frowning.

"Course she will!" explained Ziggy cheerfully. "She's bound to! Then you back off. She sits there. Then, when she slams down the lid of her desk like she always does to annoy Mr Gayle – bingo! She's in trouble! Now hurry up and give me a hand with the rest of these bolts."

But Robbie wasn't listening. He'd had enough. His blazer was covered in turpentine and yellow paint, his new strides were torn, and now Ziggy wanted him to risk a run-in with Imelda just to ensure that she sat in the right desk. Why had he ever opened his big mouth, he wondered, as he walked around the empty science classroom, searching for a rag to wipe his jacket and a safety-pin for his trousers. Ziggy returned to loosening the bolts and screws in the desk.

Suddenly, a gasp from Robbie made him look up. Robbie was looking inside Mr Gayle's desk. He held up a bunch of papers.

"Ziggy, it's the questions for tomorrow's chemistry mocks," said Robbie, with a broad grin. "Do you know how much swotting this is going to save us tonight? All we need do is take one of those home, check up on the answers and tomorrow's exam is a piece of cake."

"Then do it," said Ziggy, "we haven't much time. We've only a couple of minutes before school starts again and we've got to get these tools back in Griffiths' shed."

Robbie stuffed one of the examination papers in his top pocket, whilst Ziggy picked up loose nuts and screws and put them gently into the desk he had been sabotaging. Then the two of them hurried out of the room and down the corridor to the stairs. However, as they rounded the corner they ran straight into Mr Gayle. The science master frowned and his nose wrinkled up as he looked at them.

"Where are you two going in such a hurry?" he demanded.

"Sorry, sir!" exclaimed Ziggy, "but we haven't time to explain now. We're on an errand for Mrs McClusky. We've got to take a message down to Mr Griffiths."

"All right then," said Mr Gayle, still eyeing them suspiciously as he turned away, "get on with it!"

Both Ziggy and Robbie breathed a sigh of relief as he disappeared.

"You think he believed you?" asked Robbie.

"Who cares?" said Ziggy. "If he bothers to check up on it then we just have to invent another story. Meanwhile let's get these tools back in Griffiths' shed."

"How are we going to do that?" asked Robbie. "You don't think I'm going to go through that window again, do you?"

"No need," said Ziggy, quite carried away by the success of their lunchtime scheming, "I've got a plan."

"I was afraid you might have," said Robbie gloomily.

"Look, it's simple," said Ziggy. "I knock on the door . . . when Griffiths answers it, I distract his attention. Whilst I'm talking to him, you slip past and put the tools back. Couldn't be easier."

"Yes it could," said Robbie. "I could talk to him whilst you take the tools back. I'm tired of taking all the risks."

"Okay," said Ziggy with a grin, "if you prefer it that way then that's the way that we'll do it. But we've got to be quick about it, the bell will be going soon."

When they reached the caretaker's shed Robbie knocked on the door.

"What do you want?" asked Mr Griffiths grumpily as he opened the door.

"I thought I ought to tell you," said Robbie, "I saw some lads mucking about with your motor mower over there."

"Over where?" demanded Mr Griffiths, stepping out of his shed. As he did so, Ziggy slipped around the corner and inside.

"There," said Robbie, pointing at nothing in particular. Mr Griffiths' eyes looked in the direction that Robbie was indicating. "They must have gone now," said Robbie. "Probably gone round the side of the school. Maybe you should go after them. You could probably catch them if you . . ."

Robbie's voice trailed off as he saw Mr Griffiths looking at him in a suspicious manner.

"'Ere," said Mr Griffiths, grasping him by the lapel and sniffing at his blazer, "what's this?"

"Oh, that!" exclaimed Robbie, brushing nervously at the yellow paint stains and then looking up at the sky. "One of those seagulls did it."

"Don't give me that," said Griffiths. "That's paint from my pots. You've been in my shed and I want to know why!"

Robbie remained silent. Mr Griffiths peered angrily at him. All Robbie could manage was a swallow and a shrug.

"All right then!" exclaimed Mr Griffiths, turning and locking the padlock on the door. "We'll go and see what Mrs McClusky has to say about this."

Inside the shed, Ziggy groaned.

Meanwhile, the rest of Ziggy and Robbie's class had gathered for that afternoon's chemistry lesson. Gonch and Trev were arguing about the upcoming Cup tie between Liverpool and Spurs. Imelda was listening to her radio. Calley and Ronnie kept trying to get Mr Gayle's attention in an attempt to get it turned off, but Mr Gayle was too busy trying to find out where Ziggy and Robbie were to pay attention to them.

"All right!" he announced finally. "Since none of you seem to know where they are, then we'll start without them. Sit down everyone. Keep quiet. Take out your textbooks. That means YOU TOO, Imelda!"

Imelda scowled at him, turned off her radio and sat down at her desk. She lifted the lid and looked curiously at the nuts and bolts inside it.

"Sir," she said loudly. But Mr Gayle did not look up. He was peering equally curiously at his own desk.

"Sir," repeated Imelda.

"Not now, Imelda," said Mr Gayle, "just put down your desk lid and get out your books."

"But, sir," persisted Imelda.

"Look," said Mr Gayle impatiently, stepping out from behind his desk and striding towards Imelda. "I told you to put down the lid of the desk and get on with your work."

"But . . ." said Imelda.

Mr Gayle snatched the desk lid from Imelda's hand and slammed it down. As he did so the desk collapsed in pieces. Mr Gayle's face turned red.

"You don't know your own strength, sir," sniggered Gonch.

"That's what I was trying to tell you," said Imelda scornfully, "someone's taken all the nuts and bolts out of my desk!"

"All right, Imelda, since neither Greaves nor Wright are here you can sit at one of their desks," said Mr Gayle in exasperation. "Doesn't anyone know where those two are?"

At that moment Ziggy and Robbie were both in Mrs McClusky's office with Mr Griffiths. Mrs McClusky looked across her desk at the three of them.

"Now let me get this straight, Mr Griffiths," she said. "You say that Wright broke into your shed, but that when you went back you found Greaves locked inside it."

"Yes, Mrs McClusky, that's right," said Mr Griffiths.

"I was looking for Robbie," said Ziggy. "I just looked in and the next thing I knew I'd been locked inside."

"I see," said Mrs McClusky. "And what have you got to say for yourself, Robert?"

"The same, Mrs McClusky," said Robbie. "I went in there looking for Ziggy. This was the first time, and Mr Griffiths locked the door behind me. I had to climb out through the window. That's how I got this paint spilt on me."

"He couldn't have done," protested Mr Griffiths, "I always lock the door with the padlock. Just like you told me to."

"Well you didn't this time," said Ziggy.

"Which time?" asked Mrs McClusky.

"The time that I told him about those lads mucking about with his motor mower," said Ziggy.

"But it was the other one who told me about the motor mower, Mrs McClusky," said Griffiths.

"No," said Robbie innocently. "That was the second time. The first time it was Ziggy. Then, when you went to mark out the playing fields you locked the door again. There was no one inside then, though, 'cause by that time I'd sneaked out through the window. I didn't know it wasn't locked, see?"

Mr Griffiths began to shake his head in bewilderment as outside, in the corridor, the bell that marked the end of the first period rang.

"Thank you, Mr Griffiths, that will be all," said Mrs McClusky, shuffling a pile of papers on her desk. Ziggy and Robbie grinned triumphantly at him.

"But what about these two?" demanded Mr Griffiths.

"You can rest assured that they shall not go unpunished," said Mrs McClusky. The smiles faded from the two friends' faces.

Later, as Ziggy and Robbie stood at the bottom of the stairs outside the door to Mr Webster's English class, Ziggy noticed Robbie's frown and punched his mate playfully on the shoulder.

"Cheer up, Robbie," he said. "What's a detention between friends? And so what if we did miss Imelda getting in trouble with Mr Gayle. At least we've still got tomorrow's exam papers, haven't we?"

Robbie looked alarmed for a moment and dabbed into the pockets of his paint-stained blazer. Then a look of relief came across his face as he pulled out the crumpled exam paper.

"Here," said Ziggy, snatching it from his grasp, "let's have a look at it. Can you imagine Windy's face when we get all the questions right?"

"But you're not going to get all the questions right," said a voice, as a hand reached through the stair railings and snatched the paper from Ziggy's hand. "I am!"

Ziggy and Robbie turned to see their precious exam paper clutched in Imelda's hand.

"Give it back, we pinched that fair and square," demanded Robbie.

"Yeah, and you try to get it back and I'll tell Mr Gayle that you did," crowed Imelda.

"Robbie," sighed Ziggy gloomily as the rest of the class arrived and filed into Mr Webster's classroom, "this isn't our day."

"Yeah," agreed Robbie angrily, looking down at his tattered, paint-stained clothes and thinking of what his mum would do to him when he got home.

Robbie was still complaining when the bell for the end of school rang. He was still complaining as he and Ziggy left the main doors together. He was still complaining when Mr Gayle stopped them by the school gate.

"Now I don't know what you two were doing in my room this lunchtime," said the science teacher.

"Us, sir?" asked Robbie innocently.

"Yes, you," said Mr Gayle.

"But we never went near your room," said Ziggy, "we were locked in the caretaker's hut all lunchtime. You can ask Mr Griffiths."

"I see," said Mr Gayle sarcastically, "then I must have imagined that I bumped into you in the corridor at lunchtime. I must have imagined that one of the classroom desks collapsed this afternoon. I must have imagined all those yellow thumb prints all over my desk and the exam papers inside it."

"What exam papers?" asked Robbie nervously.

"You know exactly what I'm talking about, Wright," warned Mr Gayle. "And I don't want you doing it again," added the science master, turning back towards them as he reached his car. "I suppose I'd better warn you for your own good. Those were last year's exam questions in my desk. This year's are entirely different. They're here, inside my briefcase, and no one is going to see them until the examination tomorrow morning."

"You know, Ziggy," said Robbie, "torn trousers, trouble from my mum, detention, all the revision for tomorrow's exam questions; it's been quite a day."

"Yeah, but it will all be worth it, won't it?" said Ziggy.

"How come?" asked Robbie, looking puzzled.

"Imagine Imelda's face when she sees tomorrow's questions," said Ziggy, with a broad grin.

TV TRIVIA QUIZ

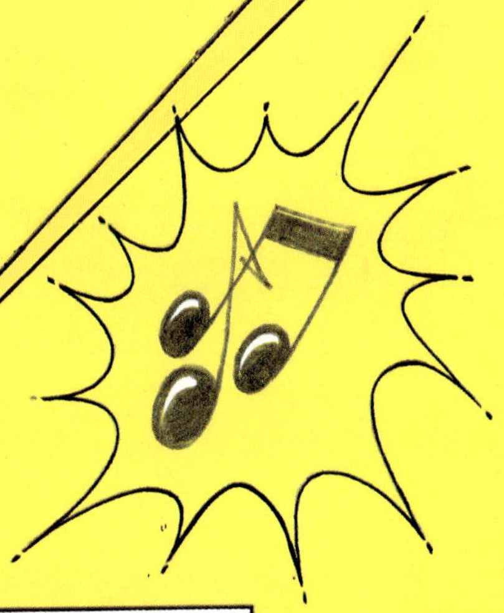

This year we've included a trivia quiz for you. The first section is about the telly, so if you get them right it means that you probably don't do enough homework. The same goes for the second section, in which the questions are all about Grange Hill. However, in the last section we've included some questions that you just might get asked in the classroom, just to give the swots amongst you a chance. After all, believe it or not, there are still eleven-point-two percent of the households in this country without a television. You can check your answers on page 60.

1 What is the longest running pop music show on British telly?
2 What have Tom, Sylvester, and Felix got in common?
3 What is the name of He-Man's twin sister?
4 What is the name of Popeye's girlfriend?
5 John Cleese, Eric Idle, Terry Gilliam, Michael Palin, Terry Jones and Graham Chapman were all members of what?
6 What is Damon Grant's real name?
7 At what time in the morning do weekday programmes of TV-am start?
8 With what programme do you associate the phrase "Come on down"?
9 Who asks the questions on Mastermind?
10 Postman Pat has a black and white what?

CHAOS IN THE KITCHEN

LATCH-KEY RECIPES FOR THE RELUCTANT COOK

It's obvious from his size that Roland likes to eat. But did you know that he liked to cook as well? Well, he does. Which is why we went to him first for a latch-key recipe – something you could make for yourself if your mum wasn't home to feed you. The only trouble was that we forgot that Roly's so keen on his food that his recipes tend to be a bit elaborate.

"Something simple," we told him. "Something with beans."

And Roly came up with Bean Burgers.

"First you need 450 grams of minced beef, salt and pepper, two tablespoons of chopped parsley, one teaspoon of mustard, some oil, four sesame seed baps, a bit of lettuce, a couple of sliced tomatoes, and loads of ketchup."

"Er, Roly," we said, "what about the beans?"

"Oh yeah," said Roly, "and a can of beans. Now you mix the minced meat with the salt and pepper, parsley and mustard. Mash the baked beans into a 'mush' and mix into the minced meat. Make into four big burgers then put in the fridge for one hour."

"Frozen burgers, Roly! You're joking?" we said.

"Hold on, I haven't finished yet. Brush the burgers with a bit of oil and grill for ten minutes on both sides. Then cut the baps in half across, put on some lettuce and slices of tomato, then the burgers, and a heap of ketchup or relish. It's great!"

Well, we thought that Roly's recipe was a little bit fattening, so we asked Gonch to give us a recipe instead. His was much simpler. All you need is a can of beans, a can opener, and a spoon. First you open the can, either clockwise or anti-clockwise, according to taste. Insert spoon in open end of tin and carefully transfer beans from container to mouth. Continue the transfer until (1) you are no longer hungry, or (2) can is empty. If (2) precedes (1) then go to fridge, locate cheese and break off corner. Break off second corner, if required. If still hungry, eat banana.

Well, that's OK in its way, but what if you want something hot? We decided to ask Danny Kendall what he could come up with. "Something hot, something lively," we told him. And Danny came up with Exploding Bean Vesuvius.

"What do you need for that, Danny?" we asked him.

"Some left over mashed potato. An egg. Some grated cheese. Some green food colouring. And some beans," said Danny. "First you pre-heat the oven to 180 degrees centigrade. Take the mashed spuds and add a few drops of green food dye."

"Why do you do that?" we asked.

"You've never eaten green mashed potatoes?" asked Danny in surprise. "They're terrific. Anyway, you take the green spuds and mould them into the shape of a volcano in an ovenproof dish. Then you fill the crater with beans. Break an egg on top and then sprinkle the grated cheese over it. Cook in the oven for fifteen or twenty minutes until the egg has set. That's all there is to it."

"Then why do you call it an Exploding Bean Vesuvius?" we asked.

"Just wait till you've eaten all those beans," said Danny.

But what happens, we wondered, if you happen to come home with some friends and there are no beans in the house? Ziggy provided the answer. You make a Huge Enormous Gigantic Sandwich.

All you really need for a Huge Enormous Gigantic Sandwich (Ziggy told us) is an uncut loaf, some butter, and some things to put in the middle.

First you cut the loaf horizontally, like so:

Then you butter it. Then you put some things in between each layer, reassemble, and then slice the whole thing vertically into the required number of slices.

We asked Ziggy what sort of things we could put in the middle. Anything you can find, he told us. Whatever you like. Cheese, pickle, cucumber, Marmite, peanut butter, slices of ham, hard-boiled eggs. Just use your imagination!

Of course there's something else you could try if none of these recipes appeal to you. You could see how much of your pocket money you've got left and then go down to the take-away!

TRIP TO THE SEASIDE

JUST IN TIME! IT'S STARTING TO RAIN!
I DON'T KNOW WHY WE COULDN'T JUST PAY FOR A SEAT, LIKE EVERYONE ELSE!
I ALREADY TOLD YOU, STUPID! BY THE TIME THEY MADE THE DRAW FOR THE FIFTH ROUND, ALL THE SEATS ON THE HISTORY TRIP HAD BEEN TAKEN. NOW SHUT UP AND GET UNDER THE SEAT!
CRIKEY, THIS IS CRAMPED! HOW FAR IS BRIGHTON FROM HERE?
ONLY SIXTY MILES OR SO, NOW SHOVE UP AND MAKE ROOM FOR ME!
SIXTY MILES! THIS BETTER BE WORTH IT, ZIGGY!
ROBBIE, WATCHING LIVERPOOL IN THE CUP IS **ALWAYS** WORTH IT!
GRADUALLY THE COACH FILLS UP...
IS THAT EVERYONE, MISTER COOPER?
ALMOST, HERE COME THE LAST OF THEM NOW.
ALRIGHT, YOU LOT, LISTEN. TODAY WE ARE VISITING THE BRIGHTON PAVILION SO I WANT EVERYONE ON BEST BEHAVIOUR. IS THAT CLEAR?
AND THE TRIP BEGINS...

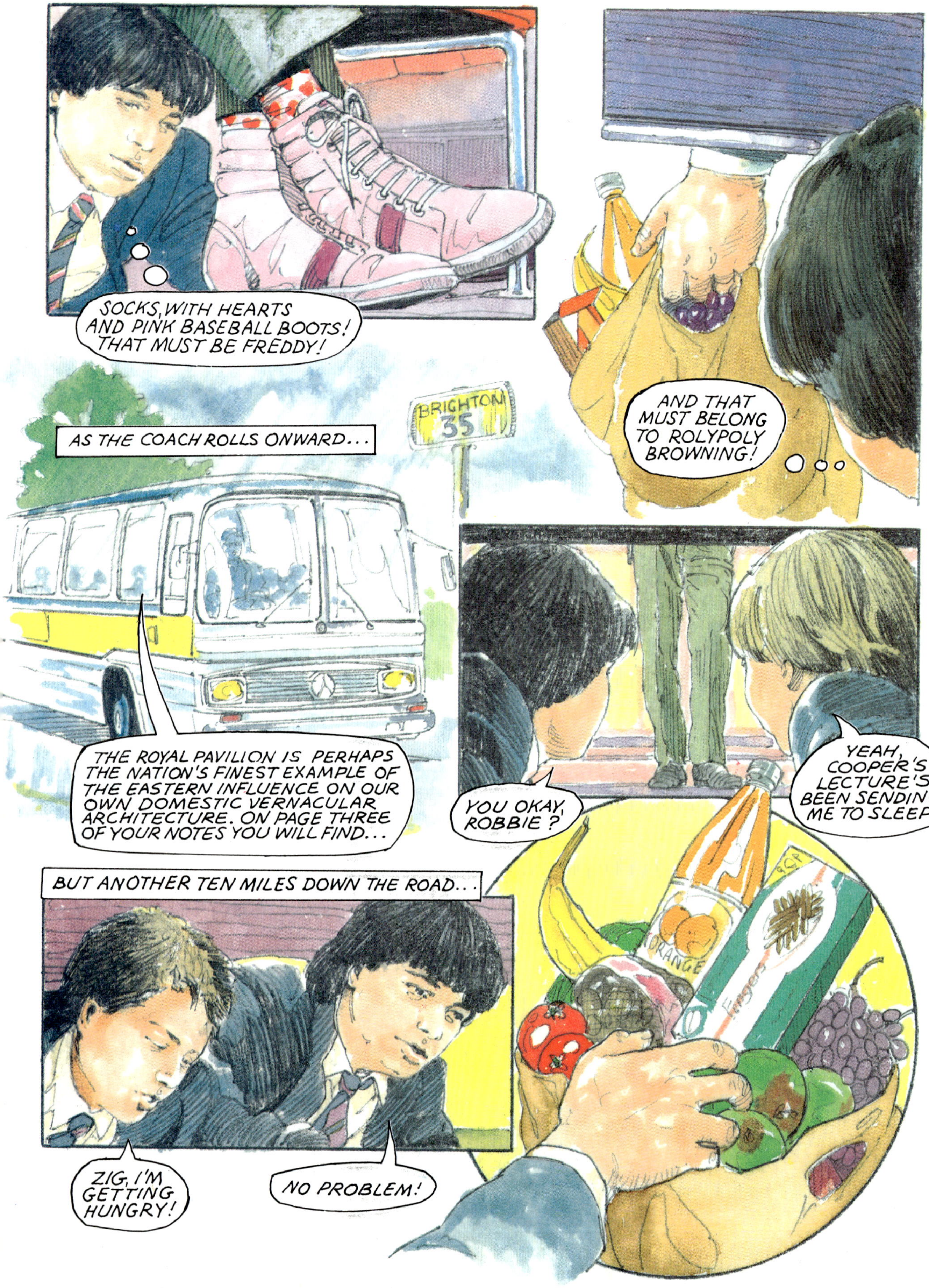
SOCKS, WITH HEARTS AND PINK BASEBALL BOOTS! THAT MUST BE FREDDY!
AND THAT MUST BELONG TO ROLYPOLY BROWNING!
AS THE COACH ROLLS ONWARD...
BRIGHTON 35
THE ROYAL PAVILION IS PERHAPS THE NATION'S FINEST EXAMPLE OF THE EASTERN INFLUENCE ON OUR OWN DOMESTIC VERNACULAR ARCHITECTURE. ON PAGE THREE OF YOUR NOTES YOU WILL FIND...
YOU OKAY, ROBBIE?
YEAH, COOPER'S LECTURE'S BEEN SENDING ME TO SLEEP!
BUT ANOTHER TEN MILES DOWN THE ROAD...
ZIG, I'M GETTING HUNGRY!
NO PROBLEM!
ORANGE
Fingers

HOWEVER...
WHAT THE HECK IS THAT?
ROLAND TAKES RETALIATORY ACTION...
STAMP!
YOUCH!
GERROFF!
AND CHAOS IS LET LOOSE...
HEY ROLY, MIND MY NEW STRIDES!
JUST COME OUT OF THERE!
I CAN'T, MY HEAD'S STUCK!
ALRIGHT! WHAT'S GOING ON HERE?
ROBBIE AND ZIGGY TELL THE TRUTH... ..ALMOST!
SORRY, SIR, WE WERE DESPERATE TO GO ON THIS TRIP!
YEAH, WE WERE DEAD KEEN TO GET A DEKKO AT THAT PAVILION THINGY!
WE'VE NO CHOICE REALLY BUT TAKE THEM ALONG, MR. COOPER.
I SUPPOSE YOU'RE RIGHT.

EVENTUALLY...
HERE WE ARE! THE ROYAL PAVILION!
IT'S HUGE, BUT WHERE'S THE CRICKET PITCH?
AND ONCE INSIDE...
THIS WAY, PLEASE.
TIME FOR US TO DISAPPEAR, ROBBIE!
BUT...
WAIT, ZIGGY, YOU WALLY! WE HAVEN'T ANY MONEY FOR THE MATCH!
WHAT ARE YOU TALKING ABOUT?
I HAD TO GIVE IT TO COOPER TO GET US INTO THE PAVILION! NOW WE'LL NEVER GET TO SEE THE MATCH!
WHERE ARE WE GOING NOW, ZIG?
I'VE STILL GOT A QUID. MAYBE WE CAN WIN ENOUGH AT THE FUNFAIR TO GET US INTO THE GAME.

BUT...
ZIG, YOU GREAT NERD! WHAT DO WE DO NOW!
WE OPEN AT EASTER
OH, STOP MOANING! I SAID I'D GET US THERE, DIDN'T I?
BUT I'M SOAKED!
AT LAST THEY FIND AN OPEN ARCADE WHERE...
CHOCKACHOCKA -CHOCKACHOCKA -CHOCK
HIRE
TAXI!
WE'LL HAVE TO BE QUICK, WE'VE ONLY TWENTY MINUTES!
HVA 691X
SEE! DIDN'T I TELL YOU!
BUT AT THE GROUND...
SORRY, LADS. WATERLOGGED PITCH. THE MATCH IS POSTPONED!
AND LATER, BACK AT THE COACH...
WHERE HAVE YOU TWO BEEN? WE'VE BEEN WAITING FOR AN HOUR!
IT'S A LONG STORY MISS!
THEN YOU CAN WRITE IT DOWN IN DETENTION, GREAVES!
AND WHEN ZIGGY GETS HOME...
ERIC! DID YOU CATCH ANYTHING?
ONLY— ATCHOO- A COLD

GRANGE HILL TRIVIA QUIZ

1 What are the names of Ziggy Greaves' two sisters?

2 Imelda Davis and Georgina Hayes were two-thirds of the Terrahawk trio. Who was the third member?

3 What is the name of the actor who plays Hollo?

4 What is the name of the school with which Grange Hill was amalgamated?

5 Mr Scott teaches what subjects at Grange Hill?

6 What is the name of Grange Hill's caretaker?

7 Julia Glover's father has a connection with Grange Hill. What is it?

8 Which Grange Hill character moved to another school after a long standing feud with Mr Bronson?

9 Gwyneth Powell plays which Grange Hill character?

10 What was the name of the donkey that lived in the caretaker's shed?

FAIR EXCHANGE

"So what did you say when he asked you out?"

"I said 'no', of course."

"Don't you like him then, Calley?" asked Ronnie Birtles, as she and her friend walked down the road that ran along the side of Grange Hill's playing fields. In the distance one of the junior classes was playing hockey.

"Well, Freddie's all right, I suppose," said Calley Donnington, running a stick along the railings beside her. "I mean, he's good fun to do the radio with and everything. But really he's just like almost all the other kids at school."

"How do you mean?" asked Ronnie, as they crossed the road, took a short cut down a footpath to the high street and then stopped for a moment to look in the record shop window.

"Exactly what I say, Ron," said Calley as the sound of Zimbabwean stars, the Bhundu Boys, drifted from the shop doorway, "they're all such KIDS. They're such show-offs. The only one I can think of who's even half grown up is Roly, and obviously no one wants to go out with him."

"Why not, just 'cause he's a bit plump? Fat people get made fun of when they shouldn't, you know, Calley."

"Yeah, I suppose you're right," agreed Calley, as they walked on, the sound of African music following them down the street, "but would you go out with him if he asked you?"

"No, I wouldn't," said Ronnie, "but that's only 'cause he's not my type."

"You mean, he's too fat," said Calley, laughing.

"No, that's not what I mean," said Ronnie. "He's not my type. He's too . . . too . . ." Ronnie stopped and looked through a rack of jeans on the pavement as she tried to think of the word she wanted. "Too sensible!" she said finally, turning from the clothes rack toward her friend.

But Calley was not listening. She was staring into the window of a shop two doors down.

"Hey, Ronnie," she said, beckoning her friend over. "Look there. Just behind the brass trays and the funny-looking pot dogs with the chains round their necks. Look at those jelly moulds. Aren't they like the ones that your mum's got?"

"Yeah, why?" asked Ronnie casually, peering into the window of the antiques shop.

"Just look at the price on them," said Calley.

Ronnie peered at the price-tag on the four jelly moulds and let out a groan.

"Fifteen pounds each and your mum's got four of them," said Calley. "I thought you'd be pleased."

"My mum USED to have four of them," said Ronnie, looking morose. "You know the jumble sale that they're having tonight to raise funds for the new science lab?"

"You mean the one that 'too sensible' Roland Browning has been organizing?" teased Calley.

"Yes, that one, but this isn't funny, Calley," said Ronnie. "Guess what I took to school and gave him today?"

"Ronnie, you didn't!" said Calley. "They're bound to get sold for fifty pence each or something like that. And just think what you could have bought for sixty pounds!"

"Just think what Mum could have done with the money," interrupted Ronnie gloomily, "after all, they were hers. And what's worse is I didn't even tell Mum I was taking them to school. I thought they weren't worth anything."

"Then we've got to get them back," said Calley. "Listen. I'll call round after tea and we'll go to the jumble sale tonight and buy them back ourselves."

"What with?" asked Ronnie.

"With the money we were going to use to go to the disco on Saturday," said Calley.

As the two girls were talking, a tall man in a tweed jacket and a purple cravat emerged from the shop doorway and picked up an elephant's foot full of walking sticks. He noticed Calley and Ronnie, and raised an eyebrow.

"What are you two doing?" he demanded.

"Just looking," said Calley. "Anything wrong with that?"

"Well there's nothing here that either of you two could afford, so why don't you run along?" said the man, carrying the elephant's foot full of walking canes into the shop and turning the sign on the door from OPEN to CLOSED.

"What an awful man!" said Ronnie.

"Stop worrying about him and get home," said Calley, taking her friend by the arm and walking her away from the shop. "I'll see you this evening, okay?"

When Ronnie got home her mum was sitting at the kitchen table doing a crossword.

"You still on a diet?" she asked Ronnie. Ronnie shook her head. "Good," said her mum. "Your tea's in the oven. Do you want it now or do you want to wait for your dad?"

"I'll have mine now," said Ronnie, helping herself to a plate of shepherd's pie. "I thought I might go out later."

"Where to?" asked her mother. "I don't want you in late."

"Oh, just to the school jumble sale," said Ronnie, and watched her mum return to the crossword. Ronnie finished her shepherd's pie and picked a tangerine from the fruit bowl on the side. "Mum," she said, as she peeled the skin from the fruit and put it in the bin. Mrs Birtles looked up. "You know those old jelly moulds you keep in the cupboard?"

"Yes," said her mum, "it's funny you should mention them. I was thinking of selling them."

"You were?" said Ronnie, not knowing whether this was good news or not.

"Yes," said her mother, "you know the shop down on the high street that that tall snooty bloke runs? Well I saw some similar in his window for fifteen pounds each so I took mine down there, and do you know what?" Ronnie shook her head. "The old skinflint would only give me ten quid for the four of them. So I told him what he could do with his ten pounds and took them home. I don't know though," said Mrs Birtles, suddenly becoming thoughtful, "perhaps I was a bit hasty. Perhaps I should have taken the money. After all, I never use them. Anyway, why do you ask?"

"Oh, no reason really," said Ronnie, getting up and switching on the kettle.

"Then try turning your thoughts to something useful, my girl, and give me two words that mean 'no robbery'. The first word ends in 'ir' and the second letter of the second one is an 'x'," said Mrs Birtles, smiling.

"Fair exchange," said Ronnie after a moment's thought.

"Ronnie," said Mrs Birtles, as her daughter went into the front room to watch the telly, "I think your dad is right. You're really not as daft as you look."

If only you knew, Mum, thought Ronnie gloomily to herself as the screen lit up with the zillionth rerun of Star Trek. Captain Kirk was just asking Scotty to 'beam him up' when Calley arrived. After talking with Mrs Birtles in the kitchen for a couple of minutes and helping her with another couple of crossword clues, Ronnie and Calley set out for the school.

As the two girls were going through the gates they met Freddie coming out. Over his shoulder were two Hawaiian shirts decorated with multicoloured pineapples.

"Neat, eh?" said Freddie. "And only fifty pence each!"

"All right if you like that sort of thing, I suppose," said Calley with a grimace. "But where did you get them?"

"From the jumble sale, of course," said Freddie.

"But I thought that wasn't due to start till half-past seven," said Calley, looking at Ronnie in alarm.

"Well, it wasn't," said Freddie. "But if you'd stayed at the radio desk this lunchtime instead of hurrying off to tell all your friends that I'd asked you out, then you'd have found out that we had to bring it forward by half an hour. The gymnasium's being used by the senior netball team later. If you're looking for any bargains, you've missed them all now."

"Freddie's right," said Banksie, joining them with a large stack of old reggae LPs under his arm. "I never knew grown-ups could get that worked up. I saw two old ladies fighting over a teapot like it was the crown jewels."

"Did you see what happened to those jelly moulds?" asked Ronnie.

"Those what?" asked Banksie, with a blank look on his face.

"Jelly moulds," said Calley. "You know, they're sort of oval shaped with lumps on the top and . . ."

"One of them was shaped like a rabbit," interrupted Ronnie.

"Oh, you mean those funny shaped old tin sandcastle buckets," said Banksie. "Roly sold them to a tall geezer in a cravat. There he is, over there."

Ronnie and Calley looked in the direction that Banksie was pointing. Beside the main doors the man they had seen at the antiques shop earlier in the day was loading a cardboard box into the back of his car. The two girls watched in dismay as he climbed into the driver's seat, and the car swept past them and out into the road.

"What did you want with jelly moulds, anyway?" asked Banksie, as he and Freddie turned and walked away together. "You're a bit old for the kind of parties where they have jelly and trifle, and funny hats, aren't you?"

"Ha, ha, very funny, Banksie," said Calley sarcastically, as she and her friend made their way towards the stairs that led to Grange Hill's gymnasium.

When they got there they found Roly, Jackie, and Zammo McGuire busy putting away the trestle tables that had been used for jumble sale stalls. In between moving the trestles, Roly was haggling with Ziggy Greaves over the price of a tattered poster of the 1976 Liverpool championship winning side. Roly wanted forty pence for it, but Ziggy was only offering ten.

"All right," said Ziggy finally, "thirteen pence and a Mars Bar. It's all I've got."

"Done!" said Roly, handing Ziggy the poster, putting the thirteen pence in the tin beside him and unwrapping the Mars Bar. When he saw Ronnie and Calley standing in the doorway, he waved to them.

"You should be proud of yourself, Ronnie," he said, smiling, as the two girls came over to him.

"Why's that?" asked Ronnie gloomily.

"Thanks to those jelly moulds you brought in, the fund for the science lab is ten pounds better off."

"You mean you sold them for ten pounds?" asked Calley.

"You must be joking!" said Roly, beaming proudly, breaking the end off his Mars Bar and popping it into his mouth. "Those were early Victorian jelly moulds, they were worth much more than that."

"Roly, how did you know that?" asked Ronnie, looking puzzled.

"There's more to me than meets the eye," said Roly, still beaming.

"And there's enough of that," said Calley jokingly.

"Make fun if you want, Donnington," said Roly. "Good things don't always come in small packages. Incidentally, Ronnie, I took the liberty of phoning your mum earlier. She said you were on your way over here, so perhaps you could give her this for me."

Roly handed Ronnie a brown envelope. Ronnie asked what was inside it. "Why don't you have a look and see," said Roly. Ronnie looked inside and saw five ten-pound notes.

"Roly!" she gasped. "What are these for?"

"For the jelly moulds, of course," said Roly. "I sold them to Mr Boxer – the man who has the antiques shop on the high street. Of course, he tried to knock me down on the price, but I knew what they were worth. In the end he gave me sixty quid. Your mum was so pleased she said I could keep ten pounds for the science lab fund. The rest is going towards your family holiday this year."

"Roly," said Ronnie, smiling, "you're wonderful!"

"Nice of you to say so," said Roly. "Have a bit of Mars Bar."

"Ronnie," said Calley with a grin, "I thought you said you didn't go for the sensible type."

BADGES RULE OK?

Gonch usually has some money-making scheme on the go. One of them was making badges. He made lots, and even sold a few – until everyone realized how quick and easy it was (and much cheaper) to make their own.

You'll need stiff card, a large safety-pin, sticky tape and non-toxic glue.

1. Cut out two card circles. Use compasses, or draw around a bottle base. A diameter of 5—6 cm is a good size. Cut out neatly.
2. Fix the safety-pin to one of the card circles. Stick the non-opening side with sticky tape.
3. Glue the two card circles together, safety-pin outermost.

THE BADGE DESIGN

The possibilities are endless, but here are some ideas to think about:

* Use coloured card. Fluorescent pinks and greens look great. Or use plain white and add a bright design.
* Use coloured felt-tip pens to spell out your name in fancy lettering. If your lettering isn't too good, use rub-down sheets of letters from art shops or stationers. They come in elaborate or plain styles, and in black or bright primary colours.
* Take a tip from Gonch. Draw one big, bold letter on each badge to spell out your name. Then wear a row of badges for your name. "That way," says Gonch, "you sell more badges. Especially if you can sell to someone like Georgina, who bought eight!" Wear on your tie or lapel.
* On a large badge with a plain white background, stick on silver and gold stars (in packets from stationers). Or draw your own stars using metallic ink felt-tips.
* Draw a bold geometric design using a thick black felt-tip on white card. Simple and very stylish.

* Design a badge to match your outfit. If you're wearing spotted leggings, wear a spotted badge to match!

* You're a Curiosity Killed the Cat fan? Let everyone know by making a badge with their name written around the edge. Stick Ben's picture in the middle.
* Make an effective mosaic badge by cutting tiny pieces of paper from colourful magazine pages and glue them onto a badge, overlapping.

SHAPES AND SIZES

Badges don't have to be round:

Make a TRIANGLE-shaped badge and decorate it to look like – a wigwam, a hat that says 'dunce', a black witch's hat for Hallowe'en, or even a cheese triangle using a stuck-on label from the real thing!

Make SQUARE badges. Cover one in brown wrapping paper, tie thin string around it and draw on a stamp and an address for a mini-parcel. Or use fancy wrapping paper and a tiny ribbon bow for a cheap and cheerful badge present.

RECTANGLES are easy to decorate. Stick a used postage stamp in one corner and write on your name and address, just in case you get lost! Or draw a piano keyboard on a long, thin badge.

If you stick to CIRCLES, decorate the badges to look like circular objects. Make a badge football, or a clock face, or a shiny apple (with a bite out!). Draw a goldfish swimming around in a round bowl, or wear two badges side by side and decorate them to look like a pair of glasses, linked by stuck-on tape. Make them as outlandish as you like – remember, you don't have to wear them on your face! Add eyes cut from magazines.

Badges can be any size:

Wear lots of tiny coloured badges grouped on a lapel. Use stiff paper and tiny gold safety-pins. Make them spell out 'I'M QUITE DOTTY'.

Wear one large badge in white card. Write a message starting at the outer edge, with the writing getting smaller and smaller as you get nearer the middle. This will drive people daft, trying to read it!

MESSAGES

Badges are great for messages. Write anything you like. How about:

WAS KILROY HERE?
ZAMMO – PHONE HOME!
GRANGE HILL RULES, OK?
HAPPY (The *H*arriet *App*reciation Society)
MR GRIFFITHS FOR PRESIDENT (of Outer Mongolia)

MEDALS

Make a medal badge. Use gold or silver metallic wrapping or art paper. Lay a piece over a 10p or 50p piece and rub with the unsharpened end of a pencil until the design shows through. Cut out and glue to a piece of card the same shape and size. Glue a scrap of looped ribbon to the back of the medal and wear the medal with a small safety-pin.

A LOGIC PROBLE[M]

WHO'S TEACHING WHO?

All you need to solve this problem is patience and common sense and a pencil.

For those of you who have never done a problem like this before, here are some tips.

Firstly, read the problem carefully and consider the clues. Then enter on the chart all the information immediately apparent from the clues using an X to show a definite 'no' and a 0 to show a definite 'yes'. For instance, Clue 2 tells you that Mr Bronson is teaching in classroom 3 so you can put an 0 in the square where Mr Bronson's line crosses classroom 3's line. From this you can tell that Mr Bronson does not teach in classrooms 1, 2, 4, or 5 and so you can put an X in each of those squares. Similarly, you should be able to work out that, since Mr Bronson is teaching in classroom 3, Miss Partridge, Mr Scott, Miss Booth, and Mr Kennedy cannot be teaching there, so you can put an X in each of those squares as well. (This has already been done for you.)

Go through each clue in turn the same way. You will find that this narrows down the possibilities and might even reveal some new definite information. So now re-read the clues with these new facts in mind to discover further positive and negative information.

Be sure to enter the information in ALL the relevant places in the chart and to transfer newly discovered information from one part of the chart to all the other relevant parts.

THE PROBLEM

Five students are studying in five different classrooms. From the clues below you can name each student's lesson, which classroom each pupil is in, and who is the teacher in each case. (To make it more difficult, for those of you who know which subjects the teachers at Grange Hill USUALLY teach, none of them are teaching their own subject!)

THE CLUES

1 Ziggy's teacher is not a man. She is not teaching history, which is in classroom 4.
2 Mr Bronson is teaching in classroom 3. (This has been filled in for you.)
3 Imelda is not studying a language and her classroom has an odd number.
4 Miss Booth does not teach science. Her classroom number is less than Miss Partridge's, who is teaching one of the boys today.
5 Danny is studying French. His teacher has a name with seven letters and teaches in classroom 5.
6 Gonch is learning English in classroom 1.
7 The science mistress is in classroom 2.

	DANNY	IMELDA	ZIGGY	HELEN	GONCH	ART	ENGLISH	HISTORY	FRENCH	SCIENCE	CLASSROOM 1	CLASSROOM 2	CLASSROOM 3	CLASSROOM 4	CLASSROOM 5
MR BRONSON	X	O	X	X	X	O	X	X	X	X	X	X	O	X	X
MISS PARTRIDGE	X	X	O	X	X	X	X	X	X	O	X	O	X	X	X
MR SCOTT	X	X	X	O	X	X	X	O	X	X	X	X	X	O	X
MISS BOOTH	X	X	X	X	O	X	O	X	X	X	O	X	X	X	X
MR KENNEDY	O	X	X	X	X	X	X	X	O	X	X	X	X	X	O
CLASSROOM 1	X	X	X	X	O										
CLASSROOM 2	X	X	O	X	X										
CLASSROOM 3	X	O	X	X	X										
CLASSROOM 4	X	X	[illegible]	O	X										
CLASSROOM 5	O	X	X	X	X										
ART	X	O	X	X	X										
ENGLISH	X	X	X	X	O										
HISTORY	X	X	X	O	X										
FRENCH	O	X	X	X	X										
SCIENCE	X	X	O	X	X										

NAME OF PUPIL	TEACHER	CLASSROOM	SUBJECT
Gonch	miss Booth	1	Engish
ZIGGY	miss partridge	2	Sciance
imelda	MR Brons	3	ART
Halan	MR Scott	4	History
Danny	mr Kennedy	5	Franch

THE ROLYPOLYBOWL

NOT THAT I'M LIKELY TO BUMP INTO HIM ANYWHERE ROUND HERE!
THEN!
WHAT THE HECK ARE THEY ?????!!!!!
WHATEVER THEY ARE, I'M OFF!
BUT...
OOOOOOOF!
BANKSIE! WHAT ARE YOU DOING ROUND HERE?
BANKSIE WAS JUST GIVING ME A RIDE HOME FROM THE DISCO, BUT DON'T TELL ANYONE, ROLY.

NEVER MIND THAT, CHERYL, LOOK WHAT HE'S DONE TO MY BIKE!
SORRY, BANKSIE, BUT THERE WERE THESE GEEZERS THAT LOOKED LIKE SPACEMEN ON THE FOOTBRIDGE!
IDIOT! IT'S JUST THOSE POSERS FROM ST. JOE'S, WHO'VE STARTED THEIR OWN AMERICAN FOOTBALL TEAM!
WHO ARE YOU CALLING POSERS?
YOU LOT! THE ONLY REASON YOU PLAY AMERICAN FOOTBALL IS THAT GRANGE HILL BEATS YOU AT EVERYTHING ELSE!
SAYS WHO?
SAYS ME!
OH, YEAH?
YEAH!
STOP BEHAVING LIKE A BUNCH OF WALLIES! IF YOU REALLY THINK IT'S A GAME FOR POSERS, THEN THE BEST WAY TO SHOW IT IS BY BEATING THEM!
NOW WHY DIDN'T I THINK OF THAT?
SEE! HE'S TRYING TO CHICKEN OUT! BE AT THE MUNICIPAL RUGB FIELDS NEXT SATURDAY OR WE'LL KNOW YOU'RE SCARED!
HANG ON, WE'VE NO EQUIPMENT, NO COACH, NO TIME TO PRACTICE!

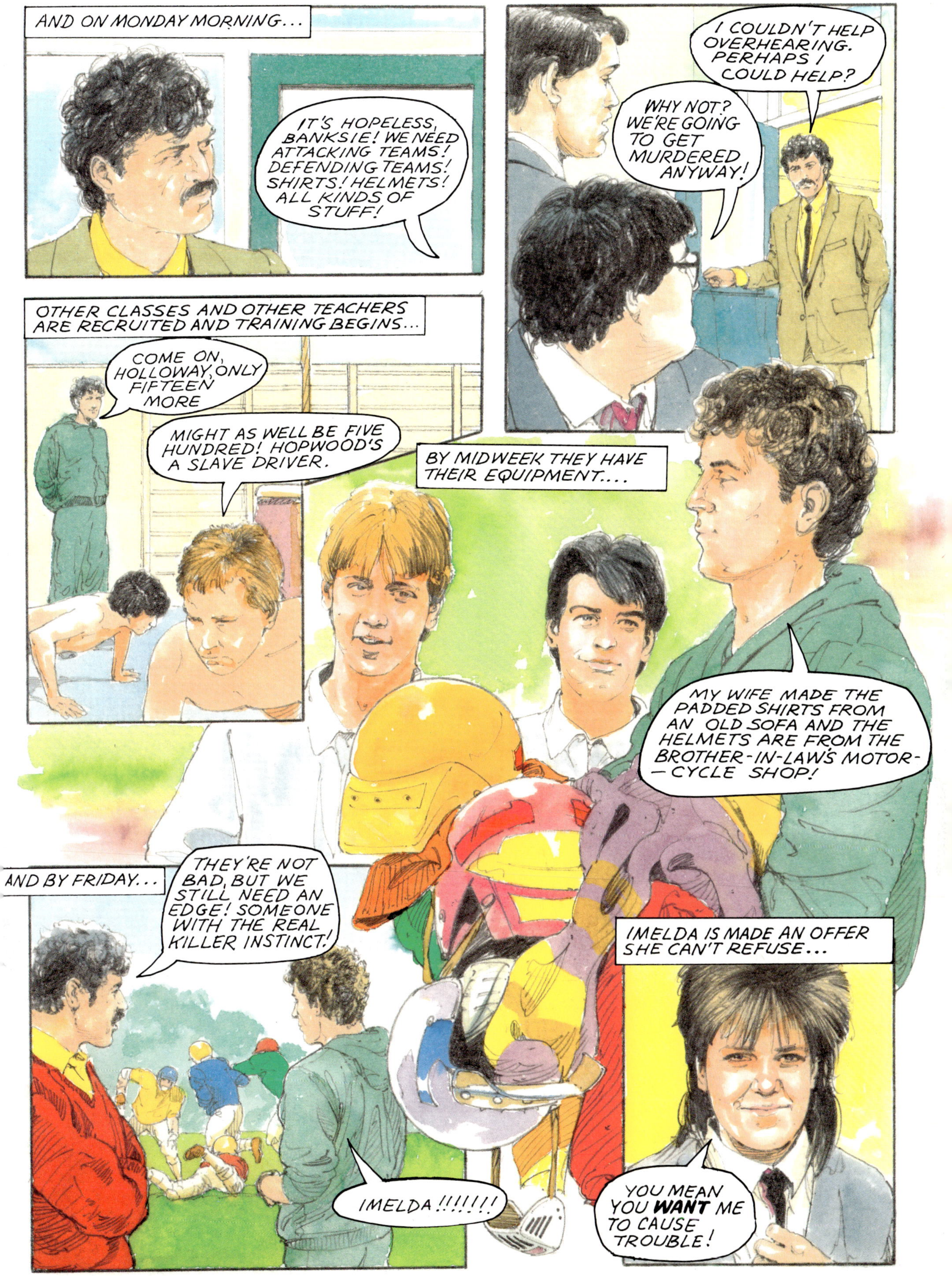
AND ON MONDAY MORNING...
IT'S HOPELESS, BANKSIE! WE NEED ATTACKING TEAMS! DEFENDING TEAMS! SHIRTS! HELMETS! ALL KINDS OF STUFF!
I COULDN'T HELP OVERHEARING. PERHAPS I COULD HELP?
WHY NOT? WE'RE GOING TO GET MURDERED ANYWAY!
OTHER CLASSES AND OTHER TEACHERS ARE RECRUITED AND TRAINING BEGINS...
COME ON, HOLLOWAY, ONLY FIFTEEN MORE
MIGHT AS WELL BE FIVE HUNDRED! HOPWOOD'S A SLAVE DRIVER.
BY MIDWEEK THEY HAVE THEIR EQUIPMENT....
MY WIFE MADE THE PADDED SHIRTS FROM AN OLD SOFA AND THE HELMETS ARE FROM THE BROTHER-IN-LAW'S MOTOR-CYCLE SHOP!
AND BY FRIDAY...
THEY'RE NOT BAD, BUT WE STILL NEED AN EDGE! SOMEONE WITH THE REAL KILLER INSTINCT!
IMELDA!!!!!!!
IMELDA IS MADE AN OFFER SHE CAN'T REFUSE...
YOU MEAN YOU **WANT** ME TO CAUSE TROUBLE!

AND AS THE TEAMS TAKE TO THE FIELD ON SATURDAY...
LOOK, THEY'VE GOT A GIRL PLAYING FOR THEM!
JUST WAIT, WIMPS!
THE TWO TEAMS ADOPT DIFFERENT TACTICS...
KEEP THE TIGHT END TIGHT FOR THE SNAP! WE'LL START WITH THE SHOTGUN AND PLAY THE RUNNING GAME FROM THE POCKET!
GONCH, YOU NOBBLE THE TALL GEEZER ON THE LEFT! I'LL TAKE CARE OF THE LOUDMOUTH WHO KEEPS SHOUTING OUT ALL THEIR ORDERS!
AND I'LL DEAL WITH THE REST OF THEM!
AND DESPITE EARLY SETBACKS...
THAT'S ST. JOSEPH'S THIRD TOUCHDOWN!
HOLLO PROVES SLIPPERY ON THE OFFENCE...
OUCH!
SOMETIMES IT HELPS BEING SMALL!
ROLY IS RESOLUTE IN DEFENCE...
SPLUNCH!
OOOOOF!

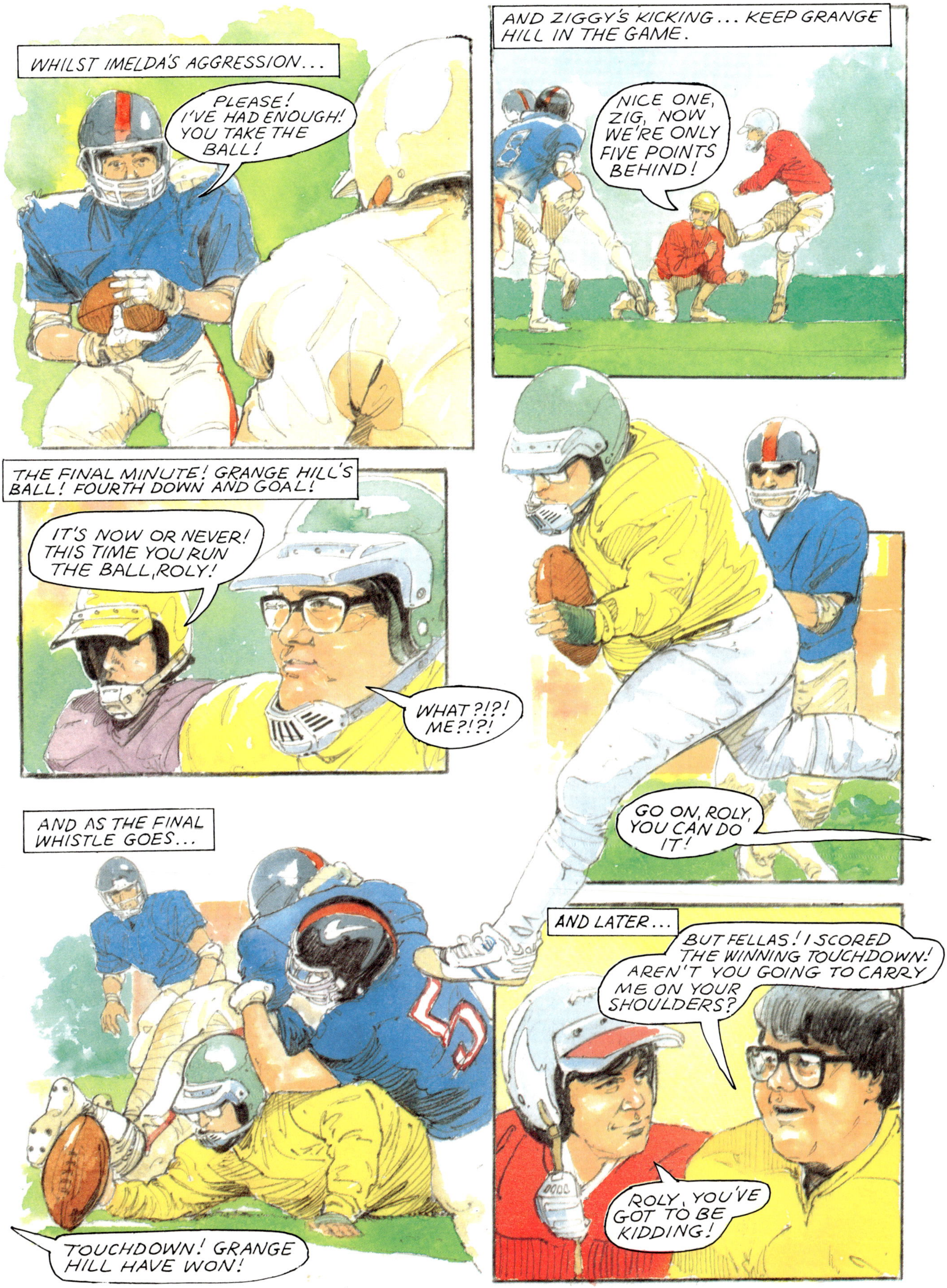

WHILST IMELDA'S AGGRESSION...
PLEASE! I'VE HAD ENOUGH! YOU TAKE THE BALL!
AND ZIGGY'S KICKING... KEEP GRANGE HILL IN THE GAME.
NICE ONE, ZIG, NOW WE'RE ONLY FIVE POINTS BEHIND!
THE FINAL MINUTE! GRANGE HILL'S BALL! FOURTH DOWN AND GOAL!
IT'S NOW OR NEVER! THIS TIME YOU RUN THE BALL, ROLY!
WHAT?!?! ME?!?!
GO ON, ROLY, YOU CAN DO IT!
AND AS THE FINAL WHISTLE GOES...
TOUCHDOWN! GRANGE HILL HAVE WON!
AND LATER...
BUT FELLAS! I SCORED THE WINNING TOUCHDOWN! AREN'T YOU GOING TO CARRY ME ON YOUR SHOULDERS?
ROLY, YOU'VE GOT TO BE KIDDING!

PLAYTIME PUZZLES

PICTURE POPS

Here are the names of ten popular bands in picture-clue form.
Can you name all ten correctly?

1

2

3

4

5

6

7

8

9

10

POSTCARD CHALLENGE

Can you step through a postcard with the help of a pair of scissors? Sounds impossible, but it's really quite easy. Try for yourself, then look at the answer and challenge a friend. Even Roly could get through!

GROOVY

How many grooves are there on a 45 rpm record?

WHAT A BARGAIN!

Jackie was out shopping with Fay one Saturday morning. "Hey, look at these dresses," said Jackie. "They've reduced them all by 30%. This one's down to £10.50. That means it was . . . er . . . the full price was . . ."

Jackie needs help! What was the price of the £10.50 dress *before* it was reduced by 30%?

THE BEATLES MAZE

Even in Liverpool Ziggy can get lost. Help him find his way through the Beatles maze.

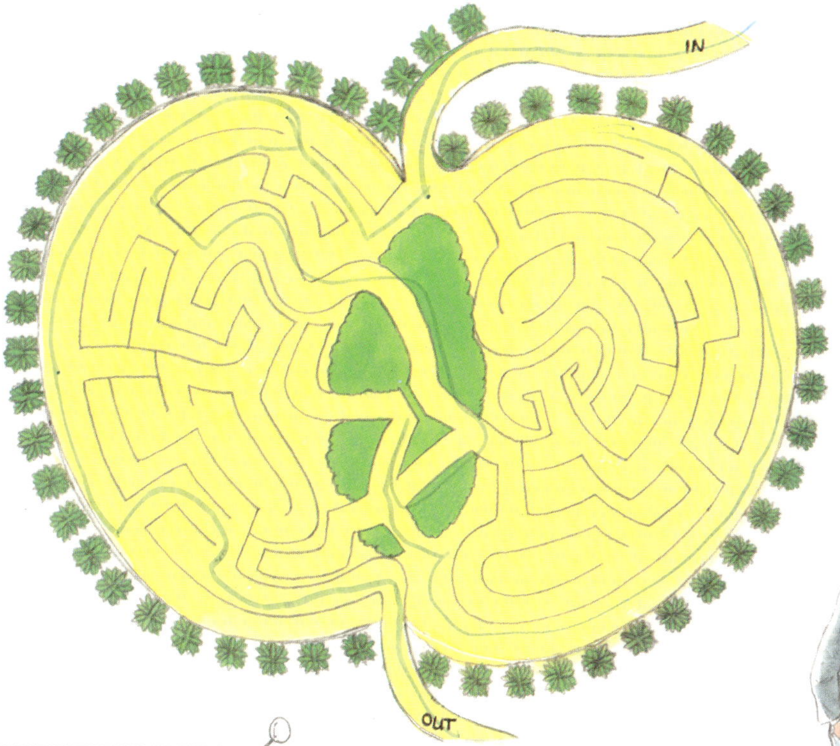

FIRST YEARS

Gonch wanted to show some of the others a match puzzle, but he didn't have any matches, so he used some first years instead! He arranged twelve of them like this, making five squares (four small and one large).

Can you take away just two first years to make two squares?

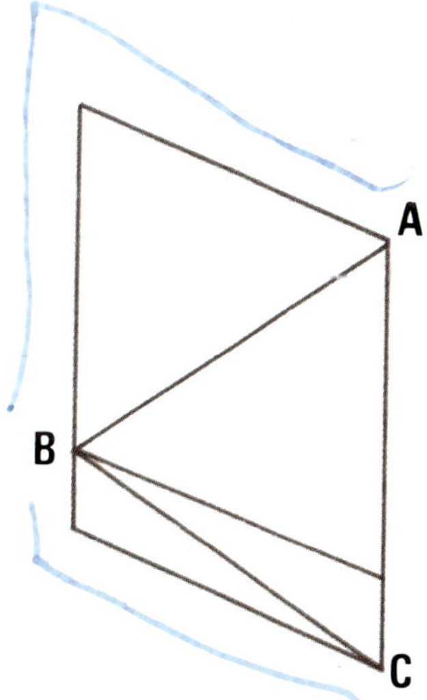

LINES

Which line is longest, A to B or B to C? No rulers allowed!

You'll find all the answers on page 60.

THE TROUBLE WITH TELEVISION

"You know, Kennedy," said Mr Spencer, as he watched Ziggy Greaves explaining to his classmates how he'd scored two goals in the under sixteens' defeat of Brookdale the previous day, "if I could get that boy to show as much enthusiasm for French Grammar as he does for football, then I suspect I'd never have to write 'Could do better' on his report card again."

"Perhaps, Leonard," suggested Mr Kennedy, "if you were a little less strict with your classes you'd get a better response."

"You mean I should throw away their textbooks, wear a clown's hat and sing them the French irregular verbs to a backing of electric guitars?" asked Mr Spencer.

"Oh, come now, Leonard, you know I don't mean that. But you could use some of the teaching aids that have been developed over the last twenty-five years, without compromising your integrity completely."

"Are you suggesting," said Mr Spencer with distaste, "that I introduce that monster, the television screen, to my classroom?"

"Why not?" asked Mr Kennedy. "The technology is already here. Why not use it?"

"Computers! Cameras! Video screens!" exclaimed Mr Spencer in disgust. "Mere gimcracks, all of them. Gimmickry! A slack and pernicious substitute for the rigours of intellectual discipline. Incidentally, I assume that the television screen in your own classroom was the source of the clattering chariot wheels and the sounds of battle that so disturbed 4F's attempts at revision for their monthly Latin test."

"Sorry, Leonard," said Mr Kennedy with a smile. "We were watching a film of Julius Caesar. It's the fifth year's set text."

"A Hollywood production, no doubt," said Mr Spencer scornfully, "with a cast of thousands and a Californian beach boy Caesar improvising his own dialogue, and scratching at his toga as if it were a torn T-shirt. Take my advice, Kennedy, stick to a sober and scrupulous study of your set texts. At least such an approach would have the advantage of being relatively silent."

"All right, Leonard," said Mr Kennedy as they reached the door to his classroom, "I take your point. I'll keep the volume down in future. If it still bothers you just knock on the pipes."

Whilst the two masters stood talking outside the classroom, Hollo was busy inside. However, the sounds of their voices, and their silhouetted shapes through the frosted glass of the classroom doorway, made him drop what he was doing and seek refuge in the tall cupboard at the back of the room. From the darkness within it he listened to their muffled voices and then silence. He was just about to open the door to see if he was safe, when he heard the sound of the door creaking open. Footsteps entered the room. Hollo remained silent.

"Hollo," called a voice quietly. It was Gonch. Hollo opened the door in relief.

"Where were you?" he demanded angrily. "You were supposed to be keeping watch down the end of the corridor."

"Sorry, Hollo," said Gonch. "I was talking to Ronnie and Georgina – they're not so bad really," he added, noticing Hollo's frown of disapproval.

"Anyway, did you get it set up?"

"Yeah," said Hollo, peering down at the two video recorders on the floor by Mr Kennedy's desk. "In fact it's almost finished."

"It looks complicated," said Gonch, looking down at the slowly revolving spools on the two recorders and the leads that joined the two together.

"Not really," said Hollo, "you set them up in synch, press one to play, one to record, and when it's over you've got your copy. Though it beats me why you want a copy of The Great Rock 'n' Roll Swindle anyway."

"I already told you," said Gonch, "it's not for me. It's for a mate of the geezer who lives around the corner from me. He collects all that old punk stuff. There could be money in it."

"Yeah," said Hollo doubtfully, as one of the cassettes came to its end and snapped onto rewind, "and it could mean trouble if we're caught, so you take the other recorder back to Miss Trethowan's room, whilst I haul the rest of this stuff back into the cupboard."

"Okay," said Gonch, picking up the video recorder, opening the door, and then peering down the corridor, "see you down the yard."

Gonch hurried down the empty corridor, the plug clattering along the ground behind him. Mr Spencer heard the sound and put his head out of the Common Room door, and caught sight of a blazer disappearing around the far corner. The plug disappeared after it, bouncing along like some tiny animal on a lead.

"STOP RIGHT THERE!" roared Mr Spencer down the corridor.

Around the corner, Gonch looked to his right and then his left. He heard Mr Spencer's footsteps coming down the corridor towards him and opened the first door that he came to. It led to the Sixth Form Room, and Gonch found himself less than welcome.

"What do you want, Gardner?" asked Banksie when he saw Gonch standing breathless with his back to the door. Outside, Mr Spencer's footsteps were approaching, and Gonch could hear him trying each door.

"I sort of borrowed this from Miss Trethowan, only she doesn't know that I did," said Gonch and handed the recorder to Banksie. "I'll be back for it later."

Before any of the sixth formers could reply, Gonch opened the door and went out.

"Did you call me, sir?" he asked innocently.

"Of course I did, boy!" said Mr Spencer. "Just what were you doing?"

"I had a message for McGuire, sir, but he wasn't there," said Gonch.

"And what did you have in your hand?"

"Nothing, sir," said Gonch.

Mr Spencer looked at him suspiciously. "Tell me, Gardner," he said eyeing Gonch more closely, "what year are you in now?"

"Third year, sir. Why?"

"That's rather old to be taking pets to school with you isn't it?"

"I don't know what you mean, sir," said Gonch, looking puzzled.

"No, of course not," said Mr Spencer, taking off his glasses and pressing his thumb and forefinger against his nose. "It's just that, for a moment, I thought that you were being followed by a tiny white frog on a lead. Now, get down to your locker and get out the books you're going to need for this afternoon's lessons."

"Roly, will you get off my toe!" pleaded Banksie from inside the Sixth Form Room. Roland, Fay, Cheryl, and Banksie were all jammed together with their ears pressed against the door. All of them had been laughing at Gonch's discomfort. Suddenly the door opened and the four of them were pushed backward in a heap. Cheryl squeaked as Roly landed on top of her. Banksie stuck his head out from the bottom of the pile and saw Mr Spencer standing looking down at them with his hands on his hips.

"I hope that you have some satisfactory explanation for this behaviour," said Mr Spencer fixing the four sixth formers with his fiercest stare.

Meanwhile, down in the playground, Hollo was waiting for Gonch. Ziggy Greaves walked past him, arguing with Mr Kennedy.

"I've told you already, Greaves," said Mr Kennedy as they passed, "the answer is 'no'!"

Ziggy looked disappointed, shrugged, stuck his hands in his pockets and then turned away. Trev

floated the Frido toward him. Ziggy caught it on his chest, and then rolled it into Vince's path.

"Hey, Vince," said Ziggy as Vince smacked the ball as hard as he could against the wall, "maybe I should ask Miss Trethowan."

"Don't you ever give up, Greaves?" asked Trev wearily.

"Course not!" said Ziggy. "Not when it's something as important as this."

Hollo was wondering what Ziggy could be planning when Gonch, out of breath and looking worried, arrived beside him.

"You get it back okay?" asked Hollo.

"No," said Gonch, shaking his head, "Spencer spotted me. I had to leave it in the Sixth Form Room."

"What about the tape?" asked Hollo.

"That too," said Gonch. "But don't worry, we'll go back after school and pick them up then."

As the bell for afternoon classes rang, Hollo wondered why he ever listened to any of Gonch's schemes. He kept on wondering all through double chemistry. And he wondered even more so when, after school, Gonch knocked on the door of the Sixth Form Room and then, getting no reply, slipped quickly inside. Moments later, holding a video cassette in his hand, a puzzled looking Gonch emerged again.

"It's gone," he said.

"What's gone?" asked Hollo.

"The recorder, you wally," said Gonch impatiently. "It's gone."

He heard footsteps approaching and jammed the cassette into his pocket. He and Hollo walked away from the Sixth Form Room and saw Miss Trethowan approaching them. Hollo swallowed nervously, and waited for the history teacher to stop them and demand to know the whereabouts of her video recorder. Miss Trethowan drew closer. Hollo swallowed again. Then, as Miss Trethowan walked past them without speaking, both he and Gonch breathed a sigh of relief.

"Excuse me, guys," said Ziggy Greaves, pushing between Gonch and Hollo and chasing after Miss Trethowan.

"Go on, Miss Trethowan," they heard him say, as he caught up with her.

"I told you already, Ziggy," said Miss Trethowan, "it's only for use for the subjects we teach. And I teach history."

"But this IS history," insisted Ziggy as they disappeared around the corner of the corridor.

"Wonder what he wants," said Hollo.

"Forget it," said Gonch. "Just think what you'll be able to do with your share of what we get for this." He tapped the videotape in his pocket.

"You know this is very illegal," said Hollo. "We could get into trouble."

"Hollo," said Gonch breezily as they walked

through the school gates together, "you worry too much. Just give me back the original tape. I'll take that back to the shop where I hired it and take the copy round to the geezer round the corner. I'll split anything he gives me with you tomorrow."

"How do I know I can trust you?" asked Hollo, as he climbed on the bus that would take him home.

"We're mates aren't we?" said Gonch, as the doors of the bus hissed closed.

However, as Gonch made his way home he started to think. He'd hired the video from the newsagent on the corner, not Hollo. And it had been him that had bought the blank tape to make the copy, not Hollo. And he'd been the one who'd nearly been caught by Spencer. And it was him that stood to get into trouble if they couldn't find out what had happened to Miss Trethowan's recorder. In fact, Hollo hadn't really done much except set up the two recorders to make a copy. Still, they were mates weren't they? Course they were, thought Gonch. If he could get twelve quid from the geezer, he'd still give Hollo two quid of it. After all, it was only fair, thought Gonch as he let himself into his house, ate an apple, and then took down the box for the video cassette from where he had left it on top of the kitchen cupboard that morning.

Gonch put the cassette into the box and then took it round to Mr Patel, the newsagent from whom he had hired it the previous evening. Then he walked home dreaming about the things he would buy with his share of the profits. It was only as he rounded the corner into his street that he realized that he'd given the newsagent the wrong cassette.

Suddenly Gonch stopped thinking about what he was going to buy. Instead he found himself thinking about just how much he could get fined for pirating videos. And if Mr Patel had found out he'd been making copies, then he could be in trouble. Gonch turned round and ran back to the shop as fast as he could. However, when he got there, he found that Mr Patel was already expecting him.

"You have made a mix-up," said the newsagent to Gonch as he pushed open the door of the shop.

"Please, Mr Patel," said Gonch holding out the newsagent's video cassette, "I never meant to . . ."

"Yes, yes, yes," said Mr Patel and took the video cassette that Gonch offered him. "'The Great Rock 'n' Roll Swindle'. Very good. Now you can have your own back. Tell me please, did you mean to push that young man into the canal?"

Gonch looked at him blankly.

"On the videotape," said Mr Patel, "you and your schoolfriends on holiday on the canal boats. It looks like good fun," he said, handing Gonch back the other tape. Gonch looked at it in surprise.

It must be the tape that the sixth formers had made of the canal holiday, he thought. But how come he had it? And if he had it, what had happened to the copy of 'The Great Rock 'n' Roll Swindle' that he had made?

The same questions chased one another round Gonch's head all evening. He could barely concentrate on his homework. What was worse, he could barely concentrate on his tea or the telly. It didn't even bother him too much to see Spurs getting knocked out of the Cup so unluckily. It was only when he got to bed that night that he realized what must have happened. He must have picked up the wrong cassette from the Sixth Form Room when he and Hollo had gone back there that afternoon. Now all he had to do was find Miss Trethowan's recorder and he'd find the other cassette. Only where was the recorder?

Gonch was at school early the next morning. He looked around the playground for Hollo, but couldn't find him anywhere. He asked Ziggy who, as usual, was playing football. Ziggy shook his head, tormented him about last night's football result, and Gonch made his way up to the Sixth Form Room where he met with his usual welcome.

"You again," said Roly, "what do you want this time?"

"This is yours," said Gonch handing him the video cassette of the barge trip. "I took it by mistake. Do you know where Miss Trethowan's recorder is?"

"Yeah," said Roly, "after we'd had a look at the barge trip we took it back to her room."

"And what about the tape?"

"What tape?"

"The tape that was in it when I handed it to Banksie."

"Oh, we put that back in it," said Roly. "Why?"

"Oh, no reason really," said Gonch, his heart sinking as he heard the bell for the start of morning school.

"Gonch," said Hollo, when he told him at break what had happened, "if brains were dominoes you'd be a double blank. I thought you said we might make some money from this."

"I don't know what you're moaning about," said Gonch gloomily. "It's not as if it's cost you anything. I've had to shell out for the hire of the video and the cost of a blank tape. And what's going to happen if Miss Trethowan puts on a tape thinking it's all about the Norman Conquest and it's Johnny Rotten singing 'Pretty Vacant'? And stop grinning, Hollo, it isn't funny."

"No, listen, Gonch," said Hollo. "It's dead simple. We just go up there this lunchtime and we take the tape. You flog it to the geezer round the corner from you, then tomorrow we share out whatever you get for it."

"Now why didn't I think of that?" said Gonch thoughtfully.

However, when they got to Miss Trethowan's classroom at lunchtime, they found that it was occupied. Miss Trethowan was setting up her video recorder for an attentive audience. The attentive audience was Ziggy Greaves.

"I suppose you want to watch as well," said the history teacher to Hollo and Gonch as they came into her classroom.

"Is that the tape that was in there last night?" asked Gonch nervously.

"Yes, why?" said Miss Trethowan.

"Then don't play it, Miss," said Hollo. "I don't think you'd enjoy it."

"Why not?" asked Ziggy. "Not everyone is a Tottenham supporter."

"What's football got to do with it, Greaves?" demanded Gonch.

"Just because your boys happened to lose to the greatest team in the world last night, that's no reason to get nasty, Gardner. If you can't stand to see Ian Rush sticking three past the Spurs defence then you shouldn't have come up here. Miss Trethowan was kind enough to record this for me because our telly has gone on the blink."

"Yes, and you can consider yourself very lucky, Eric," said Miss Trethowan, turning on the television and smiling. "I wouldn't have done it if I hadn't happened to find a spare tape that I didn't even know I had."

"But that's . . ." started Gonch, and then fell silent as he felt Hollo's elbow dig into his back.

"Come on," said Gonch turning away, "let's go and find something else to do. The last thing I feel like doing is watching Spurs lose to Liverpool. It was bad enough watching it first time round last night. Liverpool were just lucky."

"Yeah, and you lot were unlucky," said Ziggy. "Five-one unlucky."

"Er, Ziggy," interrupted Miss Trethowan trying not to smile, as, on the television screen, Brian Moore announced an hour-and-a-half's ice skating and gymnastics, "I'm afraid that you've been a little unlucky too. I appear to have taped the wrong channel."

Ribbons, Buttons & Bows

Fay likes to look fashionable and different – but being fashionable can be expensive. Why not try some of Fay's ideas to give your clothes a new look quickly and cheaply using just ribbons, buttons and bows?

RIBBONS

Ribbon comes in many widths, colours and designs. It's cheap, and it's amazing what you can do with just one metre.

* Cut a metre of ribbon in half and use it to replace boring shoelaces in your canvas sneakers or trainers. Pale blue to match denims looks good, or buy striped or spotted ribbon. If your shoes are two-colour, wear one lace in each colour. Knot the ends if the ribbon frays.

* White shirts embroidered with squiggly black cord ribbon are fashionable – and expensive. Copy the look cheaply and easily. On a basic white shirt draw a squiggly, loopy design in pencil. Using lots of the very thinnest black ribbon (or rounded hat elastic), start from a seam and stitch the ribbon in place along the drawn lines, using large black running stitches. A large area like a yoke takes quite a bit of time, so why not start by decorating the collar points, or cuffs?
* Fed-up with your half-sleeve big T-shirt? Give it a new look by tying up the sleeves in ruches. Use about a metre of ribbon for each sleeve. Pin one end at the neckline, then take the other end inside and over the sleeve till it meets up again. Tie as tightly or as loosely as you like, ruching the sleeve. Knot the ribbon, or tack in place for a more permanent look.
* Wear a thick ribbon belt with jeans. Choose a stiff ribbon the width of your belt holds, and pin in place. Tartan looks great. How much? Your waist measurement, plus about 20 cm.
* Give a loose-knit or hand-knitted jumper a new look by threading ribbon around the neck. Use a large darning needle and very thin ribbon in a matching or contrasting colour. On a V-neck, start from one side of the tip of the V, and thread the ribbon in even-sized running stitches. Make sure the ribbon lies flat. When you get to the other side of the V, stitch in place inside, or tie the ends in a neat bow. On a round neck, try adding three rows of colour-graded ribbon.
* Use the same idea to pretty-up a T-shirt or vest. Use a darning needle and thread through pale pastel ribbons for a vest neckline, or use bright colours to liven up a boring white T-shirt.

BUTTONS

Most homes have a button box or tin, and new buttons can give an outfit a whole new look.

* Add a row of large, different-coloured buttons down the front of a boring white T-shirt. Or add rows of buttons along each shoulder seam.
* Plain dresses or tops get a new look by smothering, say, the shoulder areas in a mass of many-coloured buttons, same size.
* White front-fastening blouses can be boring. Sew on contrasting buttons above and below the existing button holes for groups of three or five. Use primary reds, blues and yellows, or subtle greys, blacks and silvers.
* Replace boring buttons on dungarees with bright buttons – perhaps striped or spotted ones. Add a row of three matching buttons down the outer side seam of each leg.
* Animal buttons (sold for children's clothes) look good in groups on a T-shirt. Add lots of groups of two in a Noah's Ark line, or how about a circle of elephants, trunk to tail?

* Make a smart, sharp bow-tie and stitch to elastic to wear under a collar. If you can't tie a neat bow, CHEAT. Make a long loop, then a slightly shorter one, and hold in place with a small piece of ribbon. Stitch through to hold in place.
* Make small bows and stick them to shoes, at the front or heel. Use strong but non-toxic glue. If you don't want to stick the bows on permanently, CHEAT. Tie a piece of soft ribbon round each foot and tie in a floppy bow on top. Hide the tie by pushing down into your shoe, and pull the bow over the front. One pair of shoes goes a long way if you add ribbon bows to match different outfits.

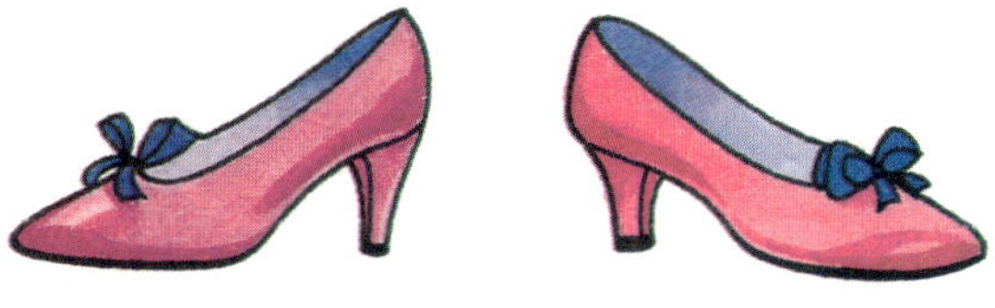

* Decorate a boring T-shirt with lots and lots of tiny bows. Using a large darning needle, thread through the fabric, and tie small lengths of ribbon into bows. Add as many as you dare! Use bright primary colours, mixed, or soft pastels.

BOWS

Bows can be simple or elaborate, casual or formal.

* Half a metre of soft, satiny ribbon makes a great hair bow. Tie at the nape of the neck, as a pony tail, or washerwoman-style on top of the head.
* If you dare, tie your hair in lots of little bunches all over your head. Using very thin ribbon, tie a bow around each bunch.
* Tie a big, floppy bow in ribbon, or any soft, floppy fabric, like cotton jersey. Stitch it to a piece of round hat elastic and wear it on top of your head, on one side, or as a bow at the neck of a shirt or blouse.

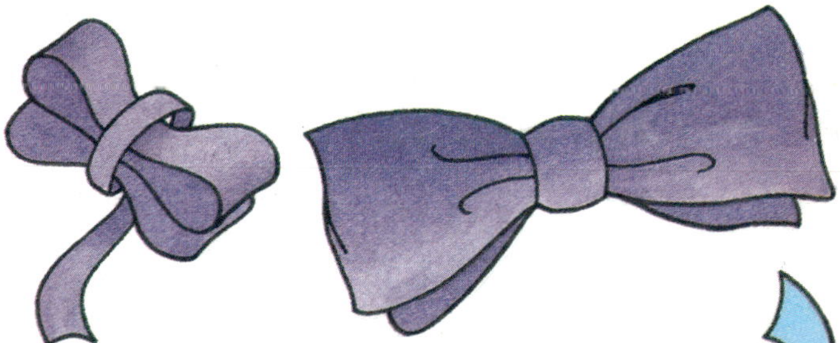

* Make tiny, tiny bows and stitch them very carefully to the back of seamed tights, one at each ankle, or in a line up to the back of the knee.

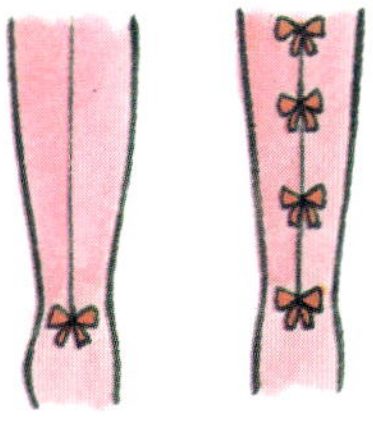

CLASSROOM TRIVIA QUIZ

1 What is the capital of Sweden?
2 Who brought the potato and tobacco to Europe?
3 What is the name of the one-legged pirate in Treasure Island?
4 How many continents are entirely in the Southern Hemisphere?
5 The numbers that we use in mathematics come from which language?
6 Sodium Chloride is better known as what?
7 What are the Australian Crawl and the Butterfly?
8 Who was the creator of Sherlock Holmes?
9 Which American city is known as The Windy City?
10 Which branch of mathematics deals with lines, points, shapes, and solids?

Robbie and the Rumour

When Gonch Gardner and Hollo Holloway had decided to take all the books out of Imelda Davis' locker for a laugh, Ziggy Greaves, who didn't usually get on with Gonch too well, had thought it was a great idea. In fact, it had been Ziggy's idea to hide them underneath Mr Stitch's car. Mr Stitch was the new addition to Grange Hill's language staff – a tall, gangling pipe-smoker with bushy black eyebrows and an ink-stained tweed jacket. He was, if anything, even more of a disciplinarian than Mr Bronson, the head of his department. When Imelda had turned up for his lesson without any of her textbooks or exercise books he had promised her two detentions if she couldn't bring her books to him by that hometime.

"But, sir," complained Imelda, "it's not my fault."

"If I had a pound for every time a pupil said that something was not his or her fault, Imelda," observed Mr Stitch, his eyebrows rising like two huge, black privet hedges, "then I would be a very rich man indeed. Your books are your responsibility. You must learn to look after them."

Imelda turned round as she heard Ziggy sniggering behind her and she glowered threateningly at him. "I'll get you at lunch for this, Greaves!" she hissed.

But even Imelda at her angriest was no match for Ziggy, Gonch and Hollo, and she was reduced to threats and accusations as the boys started a lunchtime cricket practice.

"It was you lot took the books out of my locker, wasn't it?" she demanded.

"What books?" asked Gonch.

"What locker?" asked Ziggy.

"We didn't take the books from your locker," said Hollo, "and we'll never do it again!"

Seeing the smirks on their faces, and hearing their mocking laughter, Imelda turned away angrily.

"Look at that!" exclaimed Ziggy in delight. "We really landed her in it this time, didn't we, Robbie lad?"

But Ziggy's mate Robbie Wright wasn't listening. He hadn't wanted to say anything to Ziggy or Gonch or the others, but he'd thought that their trick was a bit mean. It wasn't as if he liked Imelda or anything, but he'd never really been at war with her the way that Ziggy was. In a way he even felt sorry for her. She didn't seem to have any friends and she was always acting like a mental case. Ziggy said that that was because she WAS a mental case, but then Ziggy would say something like that. Anyway, Imelda hadn't done anything to any of them recently and, as far as Robbie could see, Ziggy had only helped hide her books so he could get in with Gonch Gardner who was claiming he could get tickets for the one-day international against the West Indies at the Oval.

"Hey, Robbie," yelled Ziggy as Robbie walked away, "where are you off to?"

"Oh, nowhere in particular," said Robbie with a shrug. "I'll be back in a minute."

"You better be," warned Trevor Cleaver, pacing back for his run up with a cricket ball in his hand as Gonch Gardner took up guard in front of the wickets. "We're supposed to be playing four innings each and they've already got one more man than us."

"All right, Cleaver, keep your hair on," said Robbie as he disappeared around the end of the science lab.

On a wall at the far side of the playing fields Imelda was sitting with a miserable look on her face.

"What do you want?" she said, scowling at Robbie as he approached.

"Look," said Robbie, "if you don't tell anyone that I told you, then I'll tell you where your books are hidden."

Imelda eyed him suspiciously. "Is this another of your tricks?" she demanded.

Robbie shook his head.

"Then why are you telling me?" asked Imelda.

"I dunno," said Robbie with a shrug. "It just didn't seem fair. They hid your books under Stitch's car. You go and get them now and you still might get out of the detentions that he said he was going to give you."

"Thanks, Robbie," said Imelda with a smile as she got down from the wall. It was the first time that Robbie had ever seen Imelda smiling and it made him feel like maybe he wasn't being an utter wally telling her where her books were hidden. In fact, she didn't look too bad when she smiled.

"Don't mention it to anyone, that's all," said Robbie.

"You know, Robbie," said Imelda, "you're not as stupid as the others."

"Yeah, and I suppose you're not as bad as people say," said Robbie blushing and smiling, unaware that Ronnie Birtles was watching them both from the bushes beside Mr Griffiths' shed.

Ronnie Birtles could hardly believe her eyes. Imelda Davis and Ziggy Greaves' best mate talking and smiling together in a quiet corner of the school grounds. Just the two of them! All by themselves! Ronnie hurried away to tell her friends what she had seen.

It was in chemistry that Ronnie told Calley, and it was in English that Calley told Jane and Sharon. And it was during history that Jane and Sharon told Helen and Georgina. And it was during the breaks between lessons that the fourths told the fifth and sixth forms. By the end of the school day the rumour that Robbie Wright and Imelda Davis had a thing going had spread all the way round the school.

"You must be off your trolley fancying her, Robbie," said Ziggy in disgust as he and Robbie walked down the school driveway together.

"I already told you, Ziggy, I don't," said Robbie. "It's just some stupid rumour invented by some twerp with nothing better to do."

"Yeah, well they say there's no smoke without fire," said Ziggy. "And where did you get to during lunchtime?"

Before Robbie could reply his elder sister Jackie fell in step beside him.

"What's this I hear about you and Imelda Davis?" she asked her brother.

"Not you as well!" groaned Robbie. "Just because you do a favour for someone doesn't mean that you . . ."

"What do you mean, 'do a favour for someone'?" asked Ziggy.

"Nothing. I said it was all just a rumour, didn't I?" protested Robbie as he and his sister climbed onto the bus that would take them home.

But Ziggy wasn't so sure. Robbie had been acting a bit funny all day. Ever since they'd had the idea to hide Imelda's books. And how come she'd managed to find them the way that she did? Maybe, for once, there was something to one of the rumours that were always floating around.

Ziggy became even more sure about his suspicions the next morning when he got to school. For once he arrived before the bell for assembly rang and he saw Robbie in the playground talking with Imelda. Imelda was giving Robbie some kind of note, and Robbie was grinning like the Cheshire cat out of Alice in Wonderland. Ziggy turned away in disgust. Moments later he felt Robbie's hand on his shoulder.

"Hey, Zig," said Robbie, excitedly, "guess what I've just been . . ."

"Don't talk to me," said Ziggy, turning away from Robbie. "I don't want to talk to anyone who's pals with that cabbage head Davis."

"But Zig," protested Robbie as the morning bell rang, "I only . . ."

"It was you told her where we'd hidden her books, wasn't it?" said Ziggy.

"Yeah, but . . ."

"And I thought we were mates," said Ziggy, walking away from Robbie.

Ziggy kept his bad mood all through morning school. Even when they divided up into their regular sides for cricket practice at lunchtime he was still annoyed.

"What do you want to play for?" he asked Robbie. "I thought you'd be talking to your girlfriend somewhere."

"All right!" said Robbie. "I'm fed up with you, with Imelda Davis, and with this whole stupid story that's got started just because I told her where you'd hidden her books. Let's go and find her. Then I'll show you!"

At that moment, Imelda was standing impatiently behind Roland Browning in the cafeteria queue.

He turned to point an accusing finger at Imelda, but she was gone. She was going to find out just who had started this rumour about her and Robbie Wright, and when she did she was going to make them sorry that they'd ever opened their stupid mouth.

She started with Georgina who told her that Helen had told her. Helen told her that she'd heard the story from Jane. Jane said she heard the news from Sharon, who in turn said that Calley told her. Calley told her that she'd heard the story from Ronnie Birtles, and Imelda caught up with Ronnie Birtles coming out of the library.

"Birtles, you're in trouble," she said, approaching with teeth gritted and a death ray stare in her eyes. "It was you started that rumour about me and Robbie Wright, wasn't it?"

"I told some mates that I'd seen the two of you together," said Ronnie defensively. "But so what? I didn't think that you'd mind. You and him seemed to be pretty friendly at lunch yesterday. What's the matter, don't you like him or something?"

"What are you staring at, Fatso?" she demanded as Roly took a slice of pizza.

"Oh, nothing," said Roly innocently, decorating his pizza with four baked potatoes. "I just thought having a boyfriend might have calmed you down a bit. I thought you might not be as mental as you were."

"What do you mean, 'mental'?" she demanded as Roly helped himself to two slices of lemon meringue pie. Roly made no reply.

All right, thought Imelda grimly to herself as Roly turned away without replying. I'll show him who's mental. Leaving her tray on the counter she strode after Roly and shoved him as hard as she could in the back. Roly stumbled and an avalanche of baked potatoes cascaded across Zammo McGuire's head. Some splashed down into his bowl of rice pudding whilst the largest of them rolled across the floor and came to rest against Mr Stitch's shiny brogue shoe.

"And just what do you think you're doing, Browning?" demanded the schoolmaster. "And don't bother telling me it wasn't your fault. You had enough food on your tray to feed the entire fifth form."

"But it wasn't my fault," protested Roly. "She pushed me."

"What business is it of yours?" said Imelda, hesitating. "And anyway I don't want anyone spreading rumours about me and him around the school."

"Okay, okay, Imelda," said Ronnie, trying not to sound too relieved, "I'm sorry. But what's the harm in it if you like him?"

"Just don't do it again, Birtles," warned Imelda as she walked away.

Maybe Ronnie was right, thought Imelda as she made her way down the corridor to her locker to collect her radio. Maybe she should try to be a little less aggressive with people. After all, Robbie had been nice to her, hadn't he? And she'd been nice to him. And it felt better than always fighting with people. Robbie wasn't so bad, she thought as she opened her locker and reached up to the top shelf for her radio. But her radio was gone.

"Is this what you're looking for?" asked a voice behind her.

Imelda turned and saw Robbie Wright holding her radio in the air. Behind him, Ziggy Greaves, Hollo, and Gonch Gardner were grinning.

"I said is this what you're looking for, cabbage head?" repeated Robbie.

"Yeah, give it here," said Imelda snatching at the radio. Robbie took a step backward away from her grasp. Then, to Imelda's surprise, she saw Robbie wink at her.

"That's no way to talk to your boyfriend," said Robbie with a sneer.

"Listen, you stupid little lame brain," said Imelda, grabbing Robbie by his tie and twisting the radio from his grasp, "I wouldn't go out with you if you were the only boy at Grange Hill. You're an even bigger twit than your mate Greaves. Anyone who says we're going together needs their head examined."

"Nice one, Imelda," whispered Robbie as he ducked underneath a wild swing of Imelda's hand. Then, as Imelda strode away from them, he turned to Ziggy Greaves. "I told you, Zig," he said triumphantly, "there's nothing between us. It was all just a stupid rumour."

"Yeah," said Ziggy, scratching his head in puzzlement. "I suppose you're right. Come on, let's play cricket."

"Speaking of cricket, Zig," said Robbie, "how do you fancy going to the one-day international next Saturday?"

"You mean you can get us tickets?" asked Ziggy.

"Yeah," said Robbie, with a grin. He didn't add that he bought them from Imelda that morning before school. Imelda had said she'd sell him two tickets that her dad had managed to get hold of and couldn't use. Imelda thought cricket was a stupid game and she could buy herself a new George Michael LP with the money if she could sell them. And since Robbie had helped her get her books back she had said she'd sell them to him if he wanted them.

"But where did you manage to get hold of them?" asked Ziggy, catching the cricket ball from Trev.

"It's a long story," said Robbie. "Remember my Uncle Charlie? Well he's got a mate whose mate's brother works round the corner from the ground . . ." Robbie paused. "You want one or not?"

"Course I do, you wally," said Ziggy.

Robbie smiled. Sometimes you couldn't tell the whole truth, he thought, not even to your best mate.

answers

TRIVIA QUIZ ANSWERS

TELEVISION TRIVIA (PAGE 13)

1 Top of the Pops
2 They are all cartoon cats
3 She-Ra
4 Olive Oyl
5 Monty Python's Flying Circus
6 Simon O'Brien
7 6.15am Monday–Friday
8 The Price is Right
9 Magnus Magnusson
10 Cat

GRANGE HILL TRIVIA (PAGE 22)

1 Allison and Michelle
2 Helen Kelly
3 Bradley Sheppard
4 Brookdale
5 Sciences
6 Mr Griffiths
7 Parent Governor
8 Ant Jones
9 Mrs McClusky
10 Harriet

CLASSROOM TRIVIA (PAGE 52)

1 Stockholm
2 Sir Walter Raleigh
3 Long John Silver
4 Two, Australia and Antarctica
5 Arabic
6 Salt
7 Swimming strokes
8 Sir Arthur Conan Doyle
9 Chicago
10 Geometry

PLAYTIME PUZZLES

(PAGES 40, 41)

PICTURE POPS

1. U2; 2. Go West; 3. The Blow Monkeys; 4. Curiosity Killed the Cat; 5. Westworld; 6. Red Box; 7. Cameo; 8. Five Star; 9. The Housemartins; 10. Bangles.

POSTCARD CHALLENGE

Cut the postcard carefully like this, open out, and step through!

GROOVY

Just two! (One on each side.)

WHAT A BARGAIN!

The dress cost £15 originally.

FIRST YEARS

Take away these two first years to leave two squares:

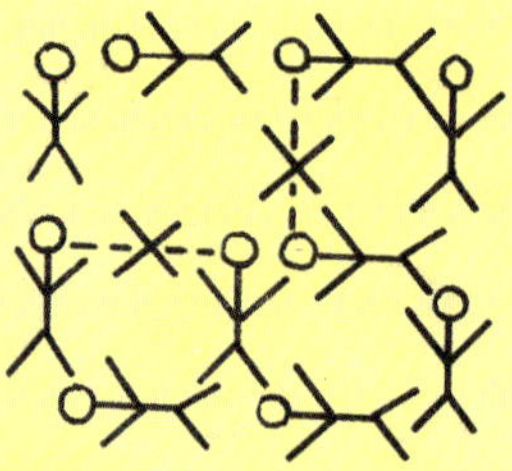

LINES

Both lines are the same length.

WHO'S TEACHING WHO? (PAGES 32, 33)

LOGIC PROBLEM BREAKDOWN

Ziggy's teacher is a woman (Clue 1). Miss Booth does not teach science (Clue 4). Therefore, Miss Partridge must be the science mistress in room 2 (Clue 7). As Miss Booth's classroom number is less than Miss Partridge's (Clue 4), then Miss Booth must be teaching in classroom 1. Danny's teacher is either Mr Bronson or Mr Kennedy (Clue 5). Since Mr Bronson is teaching in classroom 3 (Clue 2), then Mr Kennedy must be teaching Danny French in classroom 5. Since all the other teachers have already been placed in their rooms, Mr Scott must teach in classroom 4 and therefore must be teaching history (Clue 1). Gonch is learning English in classroom 1 (Clue 6). We already know Miss Booth is teaching in classroom 1 (Clue 4). Therefore that leaves Imelda in the other odd classroom (Clue 3), learning art with Mr Bronson. Helen is the only pupil left so she must be taking history with Mr Scott in room 4.

NAME OF PUPIL	TEACHER	CLASSROOM	SUBJECT
DANNY	MR KENNEDY	ROOM 5	FRENCH
IMELDA	MR BRONSON	ROOM 3	ART
ZIGGY	MISS PARTRIDGE	ROOM 2	SCIENCE
HELEN	MR SCOTT	ROOM 4	HISTORY
GONCH	MISS BOOTH	ROOM 1	ENGLISH

TEAR OUT TIMETABLE

			MORNING BREAK			LUNCH TIME			AFTERNOON BREAK			HOME TIME		
MONDAY														
TUESDAY														
WEDNESDAY														
THURSDAY														
FRIDAY														

FAY
Alison Bettles